AF880008

YOUR dfree®

for Seasoned Citizens

A Resource for Senior Citizens

Published by dfree® Global Foundation

Published by Dfree® Global Foundation, Inc.

Book Packaging: Earl Cox & Associates Worldwide

ISBN 13: 978-0-9972436-6-6
ISBN 10: 0-9972436-6-X
LCNN: Pending

Printed in the United States of America

First Edition: 2018

The information presented is intended to be general in nature and is not personal financial product and/or service advice. Accordingly, dfree®, Corporate Community Connections, Inc., First Baptist Church of Lincoln Gardens, Dr. DeForest B. Soaries, Jr., and dfree® Global Foundation, Inc., expressly disclaim all and any guarantees, undertakings and/or warranties, expressed or implied, and shall not be liable for any loss or damage whatsoever arising out of or in connection with any use or reliance on the information, material(s), product(s), service(s), and/or content presented herein.

Before acting on any information, material(s), product(s), service(s), and/or content you should consider the appropriateness of the information provided and the nature of the relevant financial product having regard to your objectives, financial situation and needs. In particular, you should seek independent financial advice and read the relevant product and/or service disclosure statement(s) prior to making an investment and/or general financial decision.

About dfree®

Founded in 2005 by DeForest B. Soaries, Jr., dfree® is a financial freedom movement that addresses the cultural, psychological and spiritual influences on financial wellness and offers practical strategies for achieving financial success. As the only faith-based, wealth-building system specifically designed with the black community in mind, dfree® delivers access to financial freedom. Visit mydfree.org for more information.

About the Founder & CEO

Dr. DeForest "Buster" Soaries, Jr. is the creator of dfree® - a transformational lifestyle movement that promotes financial freedom through values-based principles and practical approaches to financial management. The dfree® strategy, currently in use by hundreds of churches and organizations across the United States and abroad, and featured by Soledad O'Brien on **CNN's Almighty Debt**, addresses the cultural, psychological and spiritual influences on financial wellness.

Dr. Soaries is uniquely qualified to motivate and instruct people in areas of personal development and financial success. His advice is practical, his perspective refreshing and his experiences instructive. After 15 years of debt, delinquency and deficit living, he rose to become a high ranking government official, corporate director, real estate investor, author and speaker. He serves as Senior Pastor to the 5000-plus members of the First Baptist Church of Lincoln Gardens in Somerset, New Jersey, and is an independent director at the Federal Home Loan Bank of New York and Independence Realty Trust of Philadelphia. He is former Secretary of State of New Jersey and Chairman of the United States Election Assistance Commission.

Dr. Soaries is the author of ***"Say Yes to No Debt", "dfree®: Breaking Free from Financial Slavery"*** (Zondervan); ***"dfree® Lifestyle: 12 Steps to Financial Freedom"*** (UMI); and ***Meditations for Financial Freedom Vol 1 and Vol 2."*** (Faith in Action Publishing). He is President and CEO of the dfree® Global Foundation, Inc., which provides training to organizations and individuals who help people achieve financial freedom and self-sufficiency.

Dr. Soaries is a graduate of Fordham University (BA), Princeton Theological Seminary (MDiv) and United Theological Seminary (DMin). He resides in Central New Jersey with his wife, Donna and twin sons, Malcolm and Martin.

Additional dfree® Global Foundation Publications

Your dfree®: For Seasoned Citizens
Your dfree®: For Entrepreneurs
Your dfree®: For Veterans
Your dfree®: For Youth
Your dfree®: For Women
Your dfree®: For Men
Your dfree®: For Couples
Your dfree®: For Immigrants
Your dfree®: For Re-Entry
Your dfree®: For Young Adults
Your dfree®: For Community

Books by our Founder & CEO, Dr. DeForest B. Soaries, Jr.

dfree®: Breaking Free From Financial Slavery
Say Yes to No Debt: 12 Steps to Financial Freedom
dfree® Lifestyle: Say Yes to No Debt Workbook
Meditations for Financial Freedom Vol 1
Meditations for Financial Freedom Vol 2
Meditations for Financial Freedom Vol 3

Contents

WHAT IS dfree®?

dfree® is a transformational, lifestyle movement that promotes financial freedom through values-based principles and practical approaches to financial management. It was started by DeForest B. "Buster" Soaries, Jr., who is a pastor, a community developer, a civil rights advocate, a corporate director, a husband, and a father who served in federal and state and government.

If you haven't yet, you should read Soaries' *Say Yes to No Debt: 12 Steps to Financial Freedom*, which contains the dfree® principles and strategies and leads you to a life of financial security where you can give back to others. This supplement augments the book and provides information pertinent to seasoned citizens also known as seniors. You might also find more information about dfree® through your church or community organization. If your church or group doesn't have a dfree® program, perhaps you can encourage your leaders to start one.

Do you know how much debt you owe? Do you have a plan that guides your spending? Are you able to pay all your bills on time, every month? Do you have an emergency contingency income plan? Do you have enough financial resources to handle an emergency? If you answered, "no" to any of the above questions, you are a great participant in the dfree® movement.

Many seniors have joined dfree® because they have found themselves with financial questions and struggles. Maybe you never took the financial steps necessary to support your retirement. Maybe you planned well but have found yourself in debt after helping family members or friends. Or, maybe you weren't expecting to retire but suddenly found yourself unemployed or facing a major health condition. These are just some of the common experiences that leave seniors needing financial advice. dfree® can help. Others have found dfree® to be a refreshing affirmation of age old values and practices and reinforcement of strategies that have been working and will continue to work.

dfree® started in 2005 and has transformed the lives of many seniors. It is not another financial "literacy" program. It is not another "credit counseling" initiative. It is not a quick fix or a clean-up your credit campaign.[1]

dfree® is a lifestyle. It is a movement toward Financial Freedom. It's never too late to change your financial life and achieve financial freedom! dfree® believes that the road to financial freedom begins by saying yes to no debt!

dfree® is Here to Help

dfree® can be your guide to freedom from debt, delinquency and deficits. It's more than living "debt" free; it's about living free.

This movement will assist you in developing a new thought process for managing society's constant demands for instant gratification. This movement will assist you with change. Change is never simple, and it requires taking some major steps to move toward it. If you read Dr. Soaries' book, you know that the dfree® process has four stages or levels that have been effective in helping people move from constant financial stress to financial freedom. These four levels represent the exact same process that Dr. Soaries and countless numbers of others used to achieve their financial success. The dfree® movement provides all the necessary steps to initiate the change you will need to live a dfree® lifestyle.

dfree® is organized into practical steps to guide you from your initial debt, delinquency and deficit state to NO debt, NO delinquencies, and NO deficits. There are four main components needed:

1. Get Started – change the way you think
2. Get Control – take one small step at a time
3. Get Ahead – have more than you ever imagined
4. Give Back - help someone else achieve financial freedom

[1] dfree® Financial Freedom Movement_Aboutdfree. (n.d.) Retrieved 7 Oct 2016 from http://mydfree.org/about/

Level 1: GET STARTED

The goal, in this first level, is to introduce you to the basics of reclaiming financial responsibility as the key to freedom. By facing the full reality of your financial "dis-ease," you can gain an objective perspective on how your problem has snowballed and how to change course. When you admit the problem and assess your current status, you've then paved the way for changing your attitude -- the ultimate crucial step in level one.

Getting Down to Brass Tacks by Facing Your Financial Reality

What are your current financial challenges, goals and visions? The National Council on Aging (NCOA) provides resources to assist seniors with understanding and managing debt. The Federal Deposit Insurance Corporation (FDIC) provides a full curriculum that addresses frauds and scams that target senior citizens. There are many articles, books, podcasts and websites that address the many challenges of seniors as it relates to finances, including the issue of long-term care.

Lots of Seniors Are in Debt

⚠ **BEWARE:** Many, many companies target seniors with very attractive and convincing marketing materials that lure them into deeper and deeper debt. SUGGESTION: Don't even open the envelope or accept the phone call from someone offering a new loan, credit card or financial product.

A NCOA study asked professionals who work with seniors, "How does debt impact senior adults' economic security?" The study discovered many seniors are challenged by their mortgages, medical, credit card, utility and other bills, payday and other loans and back taxes.[2]

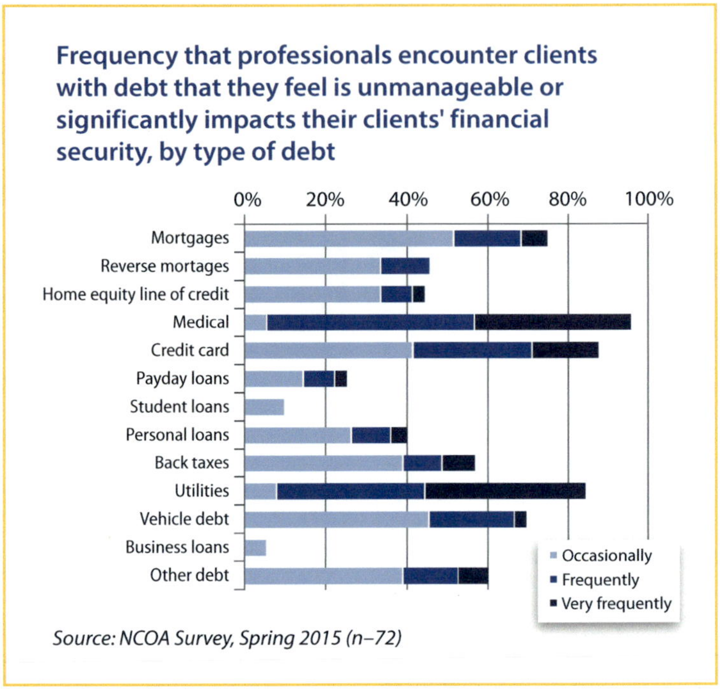

Figure 1: Debt Frequency by Type, *NCOA 2015 Survey*

In particular, many seniors are challenged by medical, utility and credit card debt. Please note that in Figure 1 the light blue represents *occasionally*; therefore mortgages, back taxes, vehicle and other debt carry a high percentage of *occasional* concern but it is the three mentioned earlier that are much more concerning.

Let's place this debt into perspective related to household income. The study reveals that, overall, debt has decreased since 2010 but is still higher than previous years. Also, there has been a slow but steady increase in debt for individuals 60+. According to the Survey of Consumer Finances — a cross-sectional survey of U.S. families conducted by the Federal Reserve Board — the percentage of households headed by an adult age 60 or over with any debt increased from 44.4 percent in 1989 to 50.2 percent in 2001 to 61.3 percent in 2013.[3]

Among older adult households with debt, the survey found that:

- Median total debt increased from $9,038 in 1989 to $18,385 in 2001 to $40,900 in 2013.
- In 2013, about 1 in 25 senior households had a negative net worth, compared to less than 1 in 50 in 2001.

[2] Older Adults and Debt: Trends, Trade-offs, and Tools to Help. National Council Of Aging. 2015. Retrieved 20 Oct 2016 from https://www.ncoa.org/economic-security/money-management/debt/senior-debt-facts/

[3] Older Adults and Debt: Trends, Trade-offs, and Tools to Help. National Council Of Aging. 2015. Retrieved 20 Oct 2016 from https://www.ncoa.org/economic-security/money-management/debt/senior-debt-facts/

- Meanwhile, 18 percent of all senior households had total debt payments, including mortgages, which were one-quarter or more of their total monthly income -- up from 13.5 percent in 2001.
- One in four senior households had a credit card debt balance of at least $7,200 in 2013.
- In 2013, 2.2 percent of senior households reported taking payday loans, up from 0.5 percent in 2007.
- In 2001, just 3.1 percent of older adult households had been late for a payment. In 2013, 6.8 percent missed a payment, and 3 percent (44.1 percent of all who missed a payment) were more than 60 days late at least once.

Proportion of senior households with debt and total debt burgden

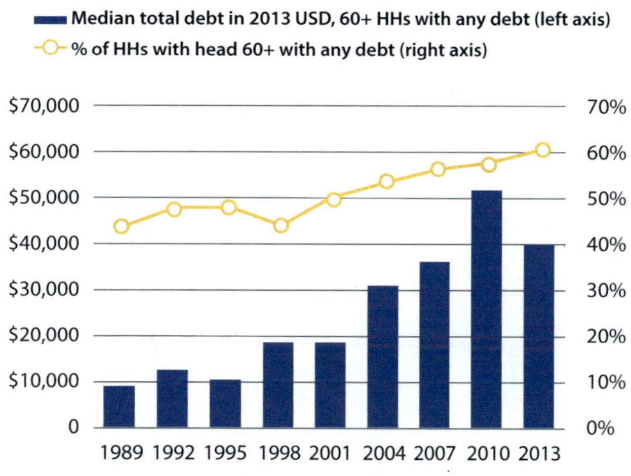

Source: Survey of Consumer Finances 1989–2013

Figure 2: Senior Debt, *Federal Reserve*

Seniors Make Significant Sacrifices

BEWARE: Don't borrow money to give other people money – especially your grandchildren!!

What is significant about seniors and debt? Many seniors are on a fixed income (pension, social security, retirement account) and have no alternative income source. Many are living off of a portion of their regular salaries but maintaining households based on previous income. Some seniors, because of deteriorating health, have encountered additional costs to maintain independent living. These seniors are struggling to alter their living arrangements for household care. Some seniors remain caregivers and supporters to other family members, including grandchildren. All of these factors and more have an impact on the quality of life for seniors.

Much attention has been focused on the decisions seniors have to make in budgeting due to the high costs of medication and food. These news stories show the hard choices individuals encounter on a regular basis. Many programs have been created to close the gaps so seniors can experience reasonable care while not compromising to sustain a basic lifestyle. Still, many seniors are making major sacrifices in trying to manage their debt and finances. In their regular (more than once per month) encounters with older clients, NCOA reports:[4]

- 23.4 percent regularly encounter seniors forgoing needed home or vehicle repairs;
- 14.9 percent regularly encounter seniors cutting pills in half;
- 14.9 percent regularly encounter seniors avoiding social engagements;
- 14.5 percent regularly encounter seniors skipping medical appointments;
- 14.5 percent regularly encounter seniors missing rent or mortgage payments; and,
- 13.7 percent regularly encounter seniors skipping meals.

Spoiling Your Grandchildren: Focus on Their Needs Versus Wants

BEWARE: Your grandchildren think you are rich! And they know that you have difficulty saying no to them. SUGGESTION: When they ask you for money, show them your budget!!!

One major source of credit card spending for seniors is buying gifts for grandchildren. While purchasing gifts for grandchildren and other family members may be done out of love or need, seniors often end up paying three to five times what the gift was worth once the credit card interest is paid. Since paying credit cards often takes years, many times the gifts are discarded or unusable by the time they are paid off.

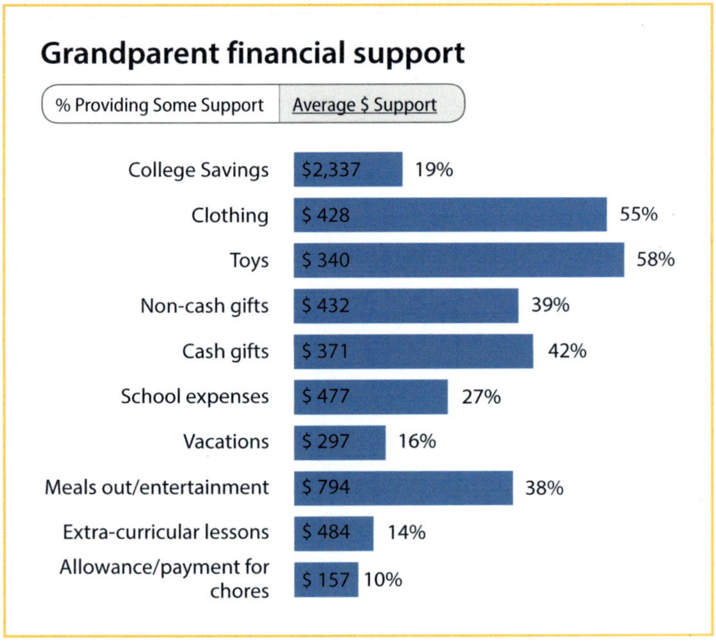

Figure 3: Grandparent Spending on Grandchildren, *TD Ameritrade*

[4] Older Adults and Debt: Trends, Trade-offs, and Tools to Help. National Council on Aging. 2015. Retrieved 20 Oct 2016 from https://www.ncoa.org/economic-security/money-management/debt/senior-debt-facts/

Some seniors come out of retirement or get second jobs so they can buy extravagant gifts for grandchildren. While this may be more fiscally responsible, you must evaluate the cost of working on your health, peace of mind, etc.

A recent T D Ameritrade survey shows that grandparents report spending an average $2,383 annually on their grandchildren (Grant, 2017).

According to an AARP study of African American and Hispanic/Latino grandparents, seniors are very involved with their grandchildren (Bittner, 2012):

	National	African American	Hispanic/Latino
Have fun with	93%	89%	86%
Teach values	83%	87%	80%
Take to cultural events	77%	72%	67%
Teach religion/spirituality	71%	79%	75%

Figure 4: Grandparent Roles, *AARP*

While some 37 percent of national grandparents in the AARP survey reported spending money on the everyday living expenses of their grandkids, percentages rose to 57 and 40 respectively for black and Hispanic respondents. Yet, grandparents of color are also less likely to deny their grandchildren just because they want, versus need, something:

	% Yes		
	National (n=1832)	**African American (n=357)**	**Hispanic/ Latino (n=371)**
Holiday/Birthday gifts	95	93	95
To help with educational expenses	53	68	58
To help with everyday living expenses	37	57	40
Because grandchildren ask for things	28	52	43

Figure 5: Reasons Grandparents Spend on Grandchildren, *AARP*

Identifying wants versus needs is a key step in becoming dfree®. You can maintain healthy and meaningful relationships with grandchildren without breaking your budget. When you make other sacrifices, such as skipping meals, to spend on your grandchildren's wants, you are not setting a good example for their financial health. Worse, you may be creating life jeopardizing situations for yourself, which also will negatively impact your grandkids.

Avoiding Scam Artists: Don't Let Unscrupulous People Take Your Hard-Earned Money

⚠ **BEWARE:** Seniors are the targets of scams of all sorts! SUGGESTION: Assume that an offer is a scam until it is proven not to be!

Older Americans, many of whom desire more interaction with others, are prime targets for scam artists. The FBI says that con artists are attracted to seniors because they tend to have nest eggs, nice homes or other desirable things. Also, even when seniors fall victim to fraud, they are less likely to report it for a variety of reasons including fear, embarrassment, lack of knowledge of how to report it and because failing memories often make them unreliable witnesses.

Even if you are somewhat technologically savvy or stay abreast of scam alerts, it's important to be ever diligent in protecting the money you have worked so hard to accumulate. If you do fall victim, the United States Senate has a Fraud Hotline, 1-855-303-9470, and online resources via https://www.aging.senate.gov/resources.

The NCOA lists the top 10 scams against seniors, https://www.ncoa.org/economic-security/money-management/scams-security/top-10-scams-targeting-seniors/, including medical insurance, fake prescription drugs and telemarketing scams. Surprisingly, NCOA reports: **"Over 90% of all reported elder abuse is committed by an older person's own family members, most often their adult children, followed by grandchildren, nieces and nephews, and others."** They recommend finding local services for seniors through the eldercare locator, http://www.eldercare.gov/Eldercare.NET/Public/Index.aspx or by calling 1-800-677-1116.

Online Financial Tools for Seniors

⚠ **BEWARE:** The computer cannot always be trusted. SUGGESTION: If you're not tech savvy, ask a grandchild or someone you trust who is tech savvy to review or set up security settings on your computer. Don't conduct financial transactions on public computers.

Instead, you need to change your lifestyle so that good financial habits become a priority. The good news is that you are not alone. As you can see from the statistics, there are many individuals who are on this journey.

Check-Up Tools

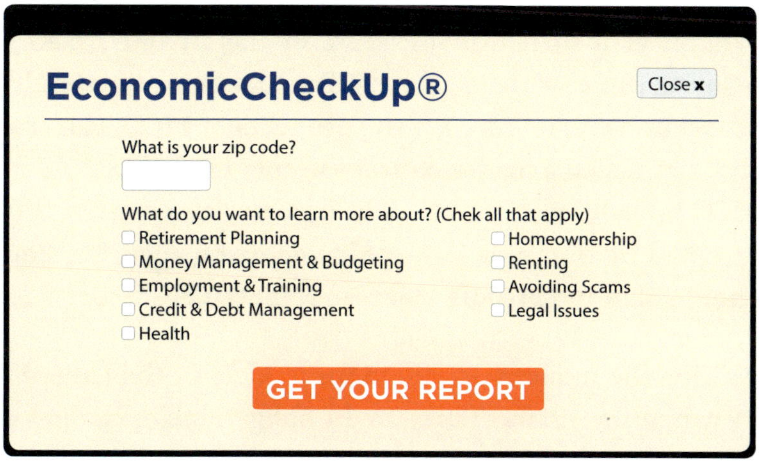

National Council on Aging has two tools created to assist you with your finances and your benefits. The *Economic Check Up*[5] - https://www.economiccheckup.org provides tips and resources to assist you with your budget, saving money, finding work (if necessary), and setting financial goals.

The other tool is *The Benefits Check Up*[6] - https://www.benefitscheckup.org, which provides links to benefit programs that could help you pay for medications, healthcare, food and more. These services are all from reliable and trusted sources.

The dfree® Financial Freedom Movement also has a variety of online tools for you to use at mydfree.com or on its Billion Dollar Challenge website at billiondollarpaydown.com

These tools will aide you in determining your current financial state and provide resources that can assist you with identifying programs and services in which you can participate.

If you don't have access to a computer or you aren't comfortable working with modern technology, dfree® has many other resources to assist you, including workshops and conferences. Following are a few dfree® tools that can assist you with identifying your current financial state. We'll start with learning more about your credit report.

[5] Economic Check Up. National Council of Aging. 2015. Retrieved 20 Oct 2016 from https://www.economiccheckup.org.
[6] Benefit Check Up. National Council of Aging. 2015. Retrieved 20 Oct 2016 from https://www.economiccheckup.org.

Get Your Credit Report Annually and Pay Attention to What's on It

REMEMBER: Your credit report can tell you if your identity has been stolen!

What is your current financial state? Has anyone stolen your identity? Do you know everyone that believes you owe them money? The first thing we should examine is your credit report. The credit report and credit score are the products of FICO, Fair Isaac Corporation, a data analytics company that developed a mathematical formula to measure one's ability to repay loans and debts. In 1981, FICO introduced the first credit bureau risk score. In 1991, the FICO's credit bureau risk score was accepted by the three U.S. credit reporting agencies, Equifax, Experian and TransUnion. In 1995, Fannie Mae and Freddie Mac also accepted FICO scores for evaluating mortgage loans.

FICO is the industry standard for lenders in the United States. The FICO® Score allows lenders to view how consumers repay credit obligations, including accounts held by other lenders. The scores are empirically built using consumer bureau data from millions of consumers. FICO® Scores are updated regularly to reflect changes in consumer behavior and lending practices (FICO, 2016).

Your credit score is derived from the information in your credit report. To understand your credit score, you have to understand what percentage of your credit habits are evaluated within your score:

Thirty-five percent (35%) of the credit score is based on your payment history. Lenders want to know if you will pay your debt. This is the most important factor of your credit score.

Thirty percent (30%) of the credit score is based on how much you owe. Lenders want to know how much debt you have.

Fifteen percent (15%) is based on the length of time you have used credit. In general, a longer credit history will increase your FICO®

Figure 6 FICO® Score summary by *Fair Isaac Corporation*

Scores. However, even people who haven't been using credit long may have high FICO® Scores, depending on how the rest of the credit report looks. Your FICO® Scores consider:

- how long your credit accounts have been established, including the age of your oldest account, the age of your newest account and an average age of all your accounts
- how long specific credit accounts have been established
- how long it has been since you used certain accounts

Ten percent (10%) examines the mix of credit; credit cards, retail accounts, installment accounts, finance company accounts and mortgage loan(s).

Ten percent (10%) calculates new credit. Research shows that opening several new credit accounts in a short period of time represents greater risk -- especially for people who don't have a long credit history.

Understanding FICO® Scores

All of the above factors create your FICO® Score. FICO® Scores generally range from 300 to 850, though industry-specific FICO® Scores have a slightly broader 250 – 900 score range. Higher FICO® Scores demonstrate lower credit risk, and lower FICO® Scores demonstrate higher credit risk. What's considered a "good" FICO® Score varies by lender. For example, one lender may offer its lowest interest rates to people with FICO® Scores above 730, while another lender only offers its lowest interest rates to people with FICO® Scores above 760.

FICO® Score	Rating	What FICO® Scores in this range mean
800+	Exceptional	• Well above the average score of U.S. consumers • Demonstrates to lenders you are an exceptional borrower
740 - 799	Very Good	• Above the average of U.S. consumers • Demonstrates to lenders you are a very dependable borrower
670 - 739	Good	• Near or slightly above the average of U.S. consumers • Most lenders consider this a good score
580 - 669	Fair	• Below the average score of U.S. consumers • Though many lenders will approve loans with this score
< 580	Poor	• Well below the average score of U.S. consumers • Demonstrates to lenders that you are a risky borrower

Figure 7: What your FICO® Score range means by *Fair Isaac Corporation*

Your credit report varies based on the credit reporting agency. The myFICO.com website explains how your credit report is compiled. All credit reports contain basically the same categories of information. Your social security number, date of birth and employment information are used to identify you. These factors are not used in credit scoring. Updates to this information come from information you supply to lenders.

Identifying Information. Your name, address, social security number, date of birth and employment information are used to identify you. These factors are not used in credit scoring. Updates to this information come from information you supply to lenders. It is important to check the accuracy of your information. Discrepancies in your identifying information could be an indication of identity fraud.

Trade Lines. These are your credit accounts. Lenders report on each account you have established. The lender reports the type of account (bankcard, auto loan, mortgage, etc.), the date you opened the account, your credit limit or loan amount, the account balance and your payment history. Please note: not all credit accounts report to the credit bureau. These factors are used in credit scoring.

Credit Inquiries. When you apply for a loan, you authorize your lender to ask for a copy of your credit report. This is how inquiries appear on your credit report. The inquiries section contains a list of everyone who accessed your credit report within the last two years. The report you see lists both "voluntary" inquiries, spurred by your own requests for credit, and "involuntary" inquires, such as when lenders order your report so as to make you a pre-approved credit offer in the mail. Voluntary inquiries are used in credit scoring.

Public Record and Collections. Credit reporting agencies also collect public record information from state and county courts, and information on overdue debt from collection agencies. Public record information includes bankruptcies, foreclosures, lawsuits, wage attachments, liens and judgments. These factors are used in credit scoring.

As the above information demonstrates, your credit report and score provide lenders with an image of who you are as a creditor. Please note: 90 percent of U.S.-based lenders use FICO to determine if individuals are qualified for credit use.

Please take time to pull your credit report. The credit reporting agencies provide a free copy of your credit report at www.annualcreditreport.com. Remember, neither your credit report nor your credit score identifies who you are as a person, it only identifies what companies have reported to the credit agencies. It is not a full picture of your net worth.

Listing Your Debt and Living Expenses

Pulling your credit report is critical as it identifies all reported debt. The credit report assists you with listing all your debt. Identifying all debt can be overwhelming yet financial freedom is most achievable when you face your reality. Create a list of all your debt, new and old. It is important to pull all your information on outstanding debt. The following worksheet can assist in this endeavor.

Auto Insurance		Household Expenses(B)		Miscellaneous Expenses (C)	
Mortgage		Home Phone		Auto Insurance	
Student Loans		Cable		Health Insurance	
Car Loan		Internet		Life Insurance	
Credit Card Debt		Water		Subscriptions:	
Credit Card Debt		Electricity		Subscriptions:	
Credit Card Debt		Sewer/Waste		Subscriptions:	
Credit Card Debt		Cell Phone		Subscriptions:	
Medical Bills		Home Security		Health Club/Gym	
Furniture Loan		Lawn Service			
Other:		Association Fee			
Total (A)		Total (B)		Total (C)	

The total outstanding debt and expenses = A+B+C $____________________

Please note: Identify the name of the card holder in the *Credit Card Debt* category. Also, list the name of the subscription (Netflix, Office 365, iTunes, etc.). Laundry, grocery and other monthly expenses were not listed but should be considered when calculating monthly expenses. This list is to identify your total cost of living.

Review your debt. Where is the bulk of your indebtedness? Is it in loans? Mortgages? Credit cards? What is causing you to be in debt? Are you willing to make the necessary sacrifices to reduce and, eventually, eliminate your debt? In order to properly focus on debt paydown, your attitude has to be in the right place.

Adjust Your Attitude: You Can Teach an Old Dog New Tricks

After 20 or 30 years or more of living in a certain lifestyle, it is certainly difficult to change. Many seniors are finding themselves more reliant upon credit cards than ever, simply to continue the lifestyle to which they have grown accustomed – yet they can't afford it. dfree® is a program that addresses the emotional and spiritual aspects of spending precisely because it sometimes takes great faith and help from above to change a hardened practice. Yet, even if you are not religious, you can benefit from dfree® by taking practical steps to curtail bad financial habits. For example, we recommend keeping a spending journal or tracking all expenses for at least 30 days to come to terms with what you actually spend money on.

Needs vs Wants

Looking at your spending, how much was driven by needs and how much was driven by wants. There are many individuals that have never taken the time to concretely distinguish between needs and wants. Too many individuals have blurred these lines so much that they cannot tell the difference between wants and needs.

Needs, defined in their simplest form, would be things required to survive: food, clothing and shelter. The definition for needs has expanded in the last century to include education and healthcare; they are no longer optional but required to survive. Needs are necessary, and we cannot live without them. Wants are defined as things desired but not necessary for survival. We need food, but no one NEEDS to eat filet mignon for dinner every night; we could survive with a hamburger patty.

Understanding needs versus wants is valuable for addressing spending habits. There are times when our wants exceed our ability to purchase, and we satisfy our wants only to discover we have caused ourselves to jeopardize a need. Example: We want a new pair of shoes. We decide to purchase a pair of $300.00 shoes, and now rent is due, and we are short $200.00. The shortage of rent causes a $150.00 late fee penalty. We need shelter so we pay the shortage plus the late fee, $350.00. We now are short on the health insurance premium of $75.00. We incur a $25.00 late fee for the insurance premium and a $35.00 overdraft fee since the payment was on automatic deposit. This cycle can go on and on. Don't allow your wants to threaten your ability to meet your basic needs.

Spending Leaks

Our spending creates habits that negatively impact our finances. We purchase some items out of habit: cigarettes, coffee, candy, chips, electronics, hair products, magazines, subscriptions, etc. These items don't cost much, but over a period you will discover you have spent more than you imagined. These expenses, on little items over time, are known as *spending leaks*. The term has been defined as expenses that utilize resources from the budget without notice or without adding value to your life (Soaries, 2015).

Maybe you don't require a cup of coffee (Starbucks, Dunkin Donuts, McDonald's) every morning on the way to work but what about pizza delivery, magazine subscriptions, premium cable or soda? These items are chipping away at your money without adding much value to your life. The value part, you may attempt to justify but, at the end of the day, WE KNOW they add little to no value. Sometimes we don't realize how much we are spending on these small items. Calculate the cost of these spending leaks for a year. If you purchased a cup of coffee ($1.49 - McDonald's) three times a week that's $4.50 a week, $18.00 per month and $216.00 per year - $2,160.00 in ten years! What could you do with $2,160? And that is without earning any interest. If you put $18.00 into an account at the end of every month that earned 5% interest, in ten years you would have approximately $2,231!! What could you do with that?

Emergencies Require Money

Spending leaks are one area that negatively impact our resources, however there are other areas. Emergencies and crises, if you have not prepared, will cause significant damage to your income and stress to your life. Emergencies happen, and the crise s will come, and if you are not prepared you could experience significant loss in addition to the emergency or crisis. What do you do when you experience an emergency or crisis? You must find a way to make cuts so that you have funds to handle the situation. The following suggested technique is not intended for routine budgeting; this technique is for CRISES ONLY!

Percentage to Cut to Create Emergency Funds

Weekly Spending	10%	$
Occasional Expenses	20%	$
Monthly Saving	50% to 75%	$
Retirement Deposit	5%	$

Increase Saving

It is necessary to know what you are spending, to identify the type of spending (needs vs wants) and to deal with crises. We must also look at our income and expenses and decide where can we cut spending so we can increase saving. Consider three action steps toward cutting spending: 1) Decide what you need; 2) Pick things to cut; 3) Make it happen.

Once you have completed this exercise, look at the results and answer the questions: Is this how I want to spend my money? Am I saving enough? Am I spending too much in areas that I can reduce? Am I using my money to help anyone?

In order to answer these questions, you need goals. For example, how do you know if you are saving enough if you don't know the end goal of your saving? Are you saving for retirement, for education, for a major need or for all three? You might not be able to make enough cuts to save for all three needs so we'll also discuss developing strategies to meet these needs. We address these issues in Level 2.

Level 2:

GET CONTROL

In level two, the goal is to develop a spending plan that accurately reflects your current reality as well as the financial freedom you long to experience. This process involves taking action and changing habits and lifestyle patterns to support your new top-priority goal of financial freedom. With a dfree® timeline in place, participants can enjoy achieving smaller goals that contribute to their ultimate objective.

As stated earlier, keep a journal of your spending for one month. Write down everything you purchase using cash, credit cards or debit cards. This will assist you in identifying the reality of your spending. However, the above table is just a snapshot of ONE month. (You'll need more space for additional months or items, but this can start your journey.)

It is our prayer that your **AWARENESS** is heightened as you read and reflect. Take ownership of your choices. If you've made poor choices, do not deflect or justify your actions. Acknowledge the difference between wants and needs. You are not the only person who has made poor choices. However, the debt that our household has accumulated generally is because of our choices.[7]

[7] Senior Debt Facts_A Profile of Senior Households with Debt. (n.b.) Retrieved 7 Oct 2016. from https://www.ncoa.org/economic-security/money-management/debt/senior-debt-facts/

While medical debt may be a major factor, usually it is not the only factor impacting senior debt. The NCOA survey reports, in 2001, approximately 27 percent of senior households held credit card balances; by 2013, more than 32 percent did.

What does this have to do with choices? Needs versus wants?

Some of our choices have a major factor on our health and our finances. It's time for a change of attitude. If you are guilty of cutting corners in an attempt to make ends meet, please make the commitment today to join dfree® for a lifestyle change.

Creating SMART Goals for Your Budget

What do you want to do to eliminate debt so you can maintain and then build wealth? Let's create a plan to determine what we need to do to accomplish the task. This plan has to be *SMART*, an acronym for Specific, Measurable, Attainable, Realistic and Timely.

In the book, *Say Yes to No Debt: 12 Steps to Financial Freedom*, Dr. Soaries, Jr., provides a percentage guide to assist you in ensuring that you come up with a practical and *SMART* monthly budget:[8]

Tithing/Giving	10%
Saving	10%
Investing/Retirement	5%
Emergency Fund	1-2%
Housing	25-35%
Utilities	5-10%
Food	5-10%
Transportation	10-15%
Clothing	5%
Medical/Health/Insurance	5-10%
Personal Discretion	5%
Recreation	5-10%
Debts	5-10%

[8] Soaries, DeForest. Say Yes to No Debt 12 Steps to Financial Freedom. Zondervan. 2015

Creating goals are important. At level one, knowing your finances is important in assisting you in creating a plan, setting a goal and identifying your financial objectives. The SMART goals assist us in determining if we are developing goals we understand, can achieve and reach.

How do you create SMART goals? It is a process of being intentional when it comes to planning and creating goals. Each time you create a goal, ask the questions: 1) Am I specific? 2) Can I measure success? 3) Is this goal attainable? 4) Is this a realistic goal, given my circumstances? 5) Is this goal timely? Can I achieve this within a given timeframe?

We need to create a plan to determine what we need to do to accomplish each goal. Virginia University created a way to assist individuals with making SMART goals, http://www.hr.virginia.edu/uploads/documents/media/Writing_SMART_Goals.pdf

Let's consider setting goals to sell a house. Let's use short-term goals to make our goals more likely to occur. We start with the following short-term goals for our home purchase:

a. Secure a real estate agent this month
b. Complete all the pre-approval paper work in 2 months
c. Identify potential homes in the areas in the third month
d. Deposit $1,000 in savings into one account each month for six-months
e. After two months, revisit budget and make adjustments to house must-haves, if the market is higher or lower than anticipated.

The chart below is an example of how to determine if your goal is SMART.

My Goal	Specific	Measurable (Define)	Attainable (due date)	Realistic	Timely
Downsize to reduce expenses	Y	At least break even	6-months	Y	Y

In the Christian bible, Habakkuk 2:2, we are reminded to WRITE the vision: "Write the vision. Make it plain on tablets so that a runner may read it." The prophet was told to write it down so others could see it, even in movement (a runner). You need to see the vision clearly regardless of where you are physically, socially or emotionally.

Make sure you write down your goals. It is always good to see what you are planning. It's a part of envisioning the future.

Place your goals some place you can see them. Don't write them down and hide them in a book or place them in a folder somewhere. Instead, post your goals where you can see them. Many people post their goals on the refrigerator, especially those associated with weight loss. Some people post their goals on their bathroom mirrors so they can see them in the morning as they prepare for their day. Some people add their goals in apps or programs on their phones. Wherever you choose to post your goals, keep them in front of you to never lose focus.

Never give up!! Whatever goal or goals you have set, do not give up. There are times when you must adjust your goals. Remember, change is the only consistent thing we have in life. Things will change, circumstances will evolve and life is filled with transitions, so be flexible to move with the flow of life.

Every goal you make and achieve leads you to another level of life's journey. Life is filled with fulfilled goals and future visons. Life in the NOW is always seeing tomorrow but maintaining your focus on today. Remember, today is the *present*. Today is our gift. Live life to the fullest.

Short-Term Goals

Decide what you want to accomplish. Maybe you need to reduce credit card or loan debt, repair something in the house, make a large purchase, payoff a medical bill, prepare for long-term care, take a much-needed vacation or just clear a bucket list item. Now that you have identified the what, consider how long it will take. Is this a goal you *CAN* achieve in days, months or years? By answering these questions, you should have the needed information to start a plan for achieving a short-term goal. How much can you cut from your budget to achieve this particular goal?

Goal: ______________________________ Amount Needed: $__________________

By: (Date) ______________________________

Things You Can Do to Save Money:

To Do:	Amount Saved
Eat out two times less each month	$
Carpool (work, shopping, gym)	$
Make sure you have signed up for Medicare if you have turned 65. Determine whether or not you qualify for Medicaid	$
Move to a smaller home	$
Try a *Staycation* vs Vacation (stay at home)	$
Don't purchase shoes or clothing for six months	$
Reduce meat and processed food purchases	$
Get rid of landline phone and just use mobile phone	$
Use ceiling fan instead of air conditioner	$
Use free internet	$
Other:	$

Now, do the actions above that you have identified as possible and then move the funds you are saving, from your checking account to a savings account.

Long-Term Goals

Below is a chart to assist with identifying your long-term goals. Please use years that make sense for you, based on your age. We begin to plan 20 years out and move on to 10 years, then 5, 3, 2 and finally create a one-year plan. List all your goals first, not in any order. Brainstorm all the things you want to accomplish in your finances, professional and family life. Rank your list based on importance to you. Describe each goal with as much detail as possible. Decide when you will start and when you will finish each goal. Below, you'll find a sample chart for 20, 10 and 5 years. We use the following goals as examples:

Financial Goals – Get out of debt, contribute to retirement, create an emergency fund, develop an investment portfolio, leave an inheritance.

Professional Goals – Continuing education, career path steps (job positions), job achievements (e.g. salary level, sales targets), professional status or recognition.

Family Goals – events with: children, grandchildren, brothers, sisters, spouse, kids. Family marriages, family vacations, family trips, family reunions, buying a second house, cottage or pool.

Life Planning Chart

20-Year Plan - Life Goals					
Financial Goals	**Goals**		**Description**	**Start**	**Finish**
	1.	Save for an emergency	Try to accumulate $1,000	2018	2020
	2.				
	3.				
Professional Goals	**Goals**		**Description**	**Start**	**Finish**
	1.	Determine what you can do that someone will pay you to do			
	2.				
	3.				
Family Goals	**Goals**		**Description**	**Start**	**Finish**
	1.	Communicate with family	Facebook Live, Facetime		
	2.				
	3.				

10-Year Plan - Life Goals					
Financial Goals	**Goals**		**Description**	**Start**	**Finish**
	1.	Payoff smallest debt first	Payoff debt using Snowball process.	2017	2020
	2.	Have written will			
	3.				
Professional Goals	**Goals**		**Description**	**Start**	**Finish**
	1.				
	2.				
	3.				
Family Goals	**Goals**		**Description**	**Start**	**Finish**
	1.				
	2.				
	3.				

5-Year Plan - Life Goals					
	Goals		**Description**	**Start**	**Finish**
Financial Goals	1.	Build an Emergency Fund	Build a fund of at least $15,000	2017	2020
	2.				
	3.				
	Goals		**Description**	**Start**	**Finish**
Professional Goals	1.				
	2.				
	3.				
	Goals		**Description**	**Start**	**Finish**
Family Goals	1.				
	2.				
	3.				

Having a life plan serves as a guide. Pace yourself when developing your plan, you don't want to become overwhelmed and frustrated. Remember, the purpose is to assist you in outlining your priorities. You can also change the areas of focus, add additional areas or delete some. This is your life plan.

Your Income	Spouse Income	Other Income	Total Income
$	$	$	$

dfree® focuses on finance. After you have identified your financial goals, create a new 7 or 14-day challenge. Remember, a challenge is a series of actions that you take every day for a set period. You decide what you want to do each day, then take that mini actions, to motivate yourself until you achieve your targeted results.

Creating a Spending Plan: Yes, You Need a Written Budget

Now that we have some concrete goals to rely upon to drive our spending plan, let's create a budget:

Household Income

Household Expenses

Monthly Bills	Occasional Expenses	Weekly Spending	Savings (remainder)
$	$	$	$

How Household Income is Spent

Monthly Bills

Expense	Amount
Mortgage or Rent	$
Phone	$
Internet	$
Television	$
Bundle (Phone, Internet, TV)	$
Water	$
Electricity	$
Garbage (Waste Mgmt)	$
Mobile Phone	$
Car Note/Bus (Commuter Pass)	$
Loan Payment(s)	$
Childcare/Tuition (grandchildren)	
Car Insurance	
Health Insurance (Supplement)	
Life Insurance	
Other Insurances	
Other Loans	
Credit Card Payment	

Occasional Expenses

Expense	Amount
Car Maintenance	$
Home Maintenance	$
Furniture	$
Medical co-payment	$
Prescription co-payment	$
Vacation	$
Clothing	$
Home/Care Assistance	$
Donations	$
Weekly Spending	
Groceries	$
Gasoline, Uber, Public	$
Coffee/Snacks	$
Dining Out (Lunch/Dinner)	$
Entertainment	$
Salon (Barber, Nails)	$
Miscellaneous	$
Monthly Total (X 4)	$

Facing Specific Challenges such as Long-Term Care

⚠ **BE CAREFUL**: You May Need Long-Term Care!!

Many seniors are faced with crises in the aging process, particularly related to the need for long-term care due to disability. The U.S. nursing home population consists of about 1.5 million individuals, most over age 85, female and widowed. And issues of long-term care may be getting worse. According to an August 2017 RAND Corporation study, the average American's lifetime risk of using a nursing home is greater than previously reported. The study suggests that, among people age 57 to 61 years old, 56 percent will spend at least one night in a nursing home during their lifetimes. The study also revealed that only about 11 percent of people in their early 60s purchase long-term care insurance due to cost and uncertainties about coverage and care.

Long-term care is expensive and unaffordable to most individuals who need this type of care. The Henry J. Kaiser Family Foundation reported that most people who need long-term care quickly exhaust personal assets and lifetime savings, so then need to rely upon unpaid help from family and friends.

Since insurance for long-term care is often out of reach for most seniors, some rely upon federally-funded programs, such as Medicaid, for their long-term care. Others rely upon out-of-pocket income through home equity, personal savings, and income from adult children.

The U.S. Department of Health and Human Services (HHS) has created a website that addresses common issues related to seniors and long-term care, http://longtermcare.gov/costs-how-to-pay/. HHS has reported that the number of seniors requiring long-term care continues to increase. The HHS website also has information about *MediGap,* which is a Medicare supplement insurance designed to fill in the gap between Medicare and long-term care.

What is the cost of long-term care? The average costs for long-term care in the United States (in 2016) were:

- $225 per day or $6,844 per month for a semi-private room in a nursing home
- $253 per day or $7,698 per month for a private room in a nursing home
- $3,628 per month for care in an assisted living facility (for a one-bedroom unit)
- $20.50 per hour for a home health aide
- $20 per hour for homemaker services
- $68 per day for services in an adult day health care center

Many seniors believe that their insurance covers long-term care. According to HHS, "Most forms of insurance, follow the same general rules as Medicare with regard to paying for long-term care services. If they do cover long-term care services, it is typically only for skilled, short-term, medically necessary care."[9]

You should make plans for long-term care; you really don't want your family to bear the burden of deciding for your care, if it becomes necessary. You may wonder how Medicare and Medicaid work with long-term care. Medicare covers the first 100 days, if the individual is hospitalized before long-term care is necessary. However, the Medicare coverage is not 100 percent. Medicare covers the first 20 days at 100 percent; days 21 to 100 the patient pays a daily deducible along the amounts of the averages noted above. MediGap insurance would pay the daily co-payment, if you have secured this insurance. Some Medicaid programs cover long-term care if the individual meets the income and medical requirements. The requirements for Medicaid vary state by state.

Please note, if you receive Medicaid for long-term care, when you move to another state, the same services may not be available. Medicaid is a joint federal and state public assistance program for financing health care for low-income people. It pays for healthcare services for those with low incomes or very high medical bills relative to income and assets. It is the largest public payer of long-term care services.[10]

Living on A Fixed Income or Social Security

While most people expect seniors to live on a "fixed income," today that term doesn't really reflect its original meaning. According to the original definition, a fixed income is "a type of investing or budgeting style for which real return rates or periodic income is received at regular intervals and at reasonably predictable levels. Fixed-income investors are typically retired individuals who rely on their investments to provide a regular, stable income stream."[11] Today, we use the term in many cases to describe income received from Social Security. Technically, the return is the investment from the years of contributing to the governmental fund. However, this may not be the source of investment that the "fixed income" phrase coiners envisioned.

[9] What Is Covered By Health and Disability Insurance. Department of Health and Human Services. Retrieved 21 Oct 2016 from http://longtermcare.gov/costs-how-to-pay/what-is-covered-by-health-disability-insurance/

[10] Glossary. Department of Health and Human Services. Retrieved 21 Oct 2016 from http://longtermcare.gov/the-basics/glossary/#Medicaid.

[11] Fixed Income Definition. Investopedia. Retrieved 21 Oct 2016 from http://www.investopedia.com/terms/f/fixedincome.asp#ixzz4NsBD9tbi

The Social Security Administration reported, in December 2015, that 60 million Americans received $883 billion in benefits. There are 40 million retired workers receiving an average of $1,342 per month. Nine out of ten individuals age 60 and older receive Social Security benefits. In 1940, the life expectancy of an individual 65 years old was 14 years; today it is 20 years. Many individuals will utilize their benefits for 20 years or more.

How do you live on Social Security benefits? Here are some helpful tips:

- Many articles and professionals stated that individuals should wait until the required retirement age, for some 66, to claim your benefits. You access 100 percent of your benefits when you wait. If you are able to wait until 70, you can increase your benefits by 32%. Each year after 66, you receive an 8% increase for waiting.[12]
- Based on the standard rule of needing 30 percent of income for your housing budget[13], the average senior can afford only $390 per month for mortgage or rent. Seniors living on Social Security should consider living with someone to share housing costs. Many seniors who own property may consider renting their property and moving into an apartment or assisted living facility for lower housing costs. Another option for property owners is to collect rent by leasing a bedroom in the house to someone he/she knows or trusts. Eighty percent of seniors live with their spouse and share the housing cost.[14]
- Where you live is important. Live somewhere with temperate climates that help you reduce utility costs. Living in a more temperate area can reduce heating and cooling costs as well as reduce the wear on HVAC systems.
- **RETIRE DEBT** before you retire. As stated earlier, set a goal to eliminate debt.
- It is imperative to stay healthy and select a reasonable health insurance. Many seniors are paying too many out-of-pocket costs for healthcare. Please research supplements to Medicare and select medical professions willing to accept the Medicare portion.
- Remember, *Benefits Check Up*, www.benefitscheckup.org? There are many programs that can assist seniors with Medicaid and health, prescription drugs, property tax relief and utility

[12] Social Security Fact Sheet. Social Security Administration. December 2015. Retrieved 21 Oct 2016 from https://www.ssa.gov/news/press/factsheets/basicfact-alt.pdf
[13] US Census Bureau. 2006 American Community Survey. Retrieved 21 Oct 2016 from https://www.census.gov/housing/census/publications/who-can-afford.pdf
[14] Coxwell, Kathleen. 11 Ideas for Living on Nothing More than Social Security in Retirement. Retirement Inc. 03 Feb 2016. Retrieved 21 Oct 2016 from https://www.newretirement.com/retirement/11-ideas-for-living-on-nothing-more-than-social-security-in-retirement/

expenses. Taping into these services may reduce out-of-pocket costs. Also consider *Eldercare Locator* http://www.eldercare.gov/Eldercare.NET/Public/Index.aspx, which provides a list of agencies providing home and community-based services

- There are many options for food and meals. Consider reducing the number of times per month you eat out. Also, when you must eat out, go to one of the many places that offer special senior days and/or reduced meal costs. Many grocery stores and supermarkets have a special day for senior discounts. Some community centers and local congregations provide meals for seniors, and some sponsor the *Meal on Wheels* program, http://www.mealsonwheelsamerica.org.

It's time to debunk the myth that seniors cannot survive on a fixed income. Yes, you can, with proper focus and a plan. Take time to review your budget, spending habits, potential cuts and determine the actions needed to move ahead.

Level 3: GET AHEAD

⚠ REMEMBER: It's Never Too Late to Get Ahead!

This level focuses on achieving the basic goals of the spending plan and maintaining fiscal health through savings, investing and real estate acquisition. As you begin to get your financial house in order, you must protect your assets, make investment decisions and enhance long-term strategies. Once you've established the basics, it's important to make sure your future is secure through retirement and estate planning, including having and maintaining health and life insurance.

It's at this stage in life we begin to consider our retirement fund, our Social Security benefits and our pension plan(s). Many of us have considered what retirement looks like or will look like however many Americans have not made adequate arrangements to retire "at ease."

Aging Towards Retirement

Prudential Insurance, one of dfree®'s corporate partners, has a television commercial about saving for retirement. They have young people draw a line to where they think one should begin saving for retirement. They have older people draw a line on where they started. The exercise revealed a huge gap between when people consider saving and when they actually start saving.

Age matters. As we age, there are some significant milestones we should keep in mind. U.S. News' article *10 Important Ages for Retirement Planning* provides an overview of things to consider at certain milestones in life, particularly retirement preparation. This article is a good guide, starting from age 50 and up: [15]

Age 50. Beginning at age 50, you can defer paying income tax on more of your retirement savings in a 401(k) or IRA. The contribution limit for 401(k)s, 403(b)s, and the federal government's Thrift Savings Plan is $22,500 for people who were age 50 and older in 2012, which is $5,500 more than younger people can deposit in these accounts. Older workers can also tuck away $1,000 more than their younger counterparts in a traditional or Roth IRA.

Age 55. Retirees who leave their jobs during the calendar year when they turn 55, or later, can make withdrawals from a 401(k), but not IRA, without having to pay the 10 percent early withdrawal penalty.

Age 59½. The 10 percent early withdrawal penalty on IRA withdrawals ends at age 59½. However, you are not required to take distributions until after you reach age 70½.

Age 62. Workers become eligible to sign up for Social Security benefits at age 62. It's important to note that your payout will be reduced if you begin payments at this age. Also, people this age who work and receive Social Security benefits at the same time could have their payments temporarily withheld if they earn above certain annual limits.

Age 65. Medicare eligibility begins at age 65. The initial enrollment period starts three months before the month you reach age 65 and ends three months after your birthday. It's a good idea to sign up right away because Medicare Part B premiums will increase by 10 percent for each 12-month period you were eligible for benefits but did not enroll.

Age 66. Baby boomers born between 1943 and 1954 qualify for the full amount of Social Security they have earned at age 66. For those born between 1955 and 1959, the full retirement age gradually increases from 66 and two months to 66 and 10 months. Once you reach your full retirement age, you will also be able to work and claim Social Security payments at the same time without having any of your payment withheld.

---

[15] 10 Important Ages For Retirement Planning. 21 Feb 2012. Retrieved 17 Oct 2016 from http://money.usnews.com/money/retirement/articles/2012/02/21/10-important-ages-for-retirement-planning

Age 67. The Social Security full retirement age is higher for younger workers. Eligibility for unreduced Social Security payments for workers born in 1960 or later begins at age 67.

Age 70. Social Security payments continue to grow by 8 percent per year for each year you delay claiming up until age 70.

Age 70½. Withdrawals from 401(k)s and IRAs become required after age 70½. If you don't withdraw the correct amount, you will be required to pay a 50 percent excise tax on the amount that should have been taken out. The first distribution is due by April 1 of the year after you turn 70½. After that, annual withdrawals will be required by December 31 each year. If you delay your first withdrawal until April, you will need to take two distributions in the same year.

The Internal Revenue Services (IRS) website identifies multiple types of retirement accounts: Individual Retirement Arrangements (IRAs), Roth IRAs, 401(k) Plans, 403(b) Plans, SIMPLE IRA Plans (Savings Incentive Match Plans for Employees), SEP Plans (Simplified Employee Pension), SARSEP Plans (Salary Reduction Simplified Employee Pension), Payroll Deduction IRAs, Profit-Sharing Plans, Defined Benefit Plans, Money Purchase Plans, Employee Stock Ownership Plans (ESOPs), Governmental Plans, 457 Plans and the 409A Non-qualified Deferred Compensation Plans.[16]

Determining which plan is right for you is left up to you and a financial profession.

Did you know?[17]

- Retirement can last for 30 years or more.
- You might need up to 80 percent of your current annual income to retire comfortably.
- The average monthly benefit paid by the Social Security Administration is $1,200.

The IRA allows anyone to contribute up to $5,500 a year to an IRA ($6,500 if you're over 50). The money grows tax-free. You can contribute to both an IRA and a 401(k). If you use a Roth IRA you are contributing after-tax dollars, and you get no tax deduction for your contribution. The money you earn grows tax-free, and you pay no tax on withdrawals after you reach 59 1/2. Plus, unlike with

[16] Types of Retirement Plans. Internal Revenue Service. (n.d) Retrieved 17 Oct 2016. from https://www.irs.gov/retirement-plans/plan-sponsor/types-of-retirement-plans-1

[17] Lots of Benefits When You Set Up An Employee Retirement Plan (n.d.) Retrieved 17 Oct 2016 from https://www.irs.gov/retirement-plans/plan-sponsor/types-of-retirement-plans-1

regular IRAs, there is no mandatory withdrawal at age 70, but you can withdraw the amount you contributed (but not your earnings) at any time with no penalty or no taxes due, which is not the case with traditional IRAs.

The 401(k), 403(b), Simple IRA and SEP Plans are all employee designed accounts. Your employer sets up these accounts for their employees. Each account is different based on the employer's requirements.

Most people believe they need at least $1,000.00 to start their IRA account, but today there are many companies that have waived or removed the initial investment requirement. There are no good excuses for not setting up a retirement plan.

It's Important to Find a Reputable Financial Advisor

Properly planning for retirement can be complicated if you are not familiar with investments and retirement accounts. We strongly recommend seeking the help and support of a professional. Too many people get their financial advice from the barber shop or the beauty shop! A financial advisor and a financial planner are individuals who can assist you with your investments and understanding the pros and cons of retirement plans. Also, consider consulting with a tax advisor, the financial expert with advanced training and knowledge of tax law, such as a certified public accountant (CPA), tax attorney or a specialized financial advisor. [18]

How do you find a reputable financial advisor? Remember, the community is the source of much of what we do. Ask your friends, co-workers, family and church members for recommendations. Financial advisors are either commissioned or non-commissioned, so you should decide if you want to work with someone on commission or non-commission. A commissioned advisor is compensated by the products he/she sells while a non-commissioned advisor charges a retainer rate or by the hour. Know what type of service you want from the advisor. Are you looking for someone to manage your financial portfolio or do you need someone to answer questions you may have from time to time? What standard of compliance does the advisor adhere to, fiduciary or suitability? What license does he/she hold?

"There are two standards of compliance in the financial industry, fiduciary and suitability," says

[18] Tax Advisor Definition | Investopedia http://www.investopedia.com/terms/t/taxadvisor.asp#ixzz4NLLjslaw

Steve Lewit, CEO and founder of Wealth Financial Group in Illinois. “Advisors who carry a fiduciary responsibility are legally bound to do the very best for you, to put you first in all their planning and product selection. A financial professional who has a suitability requirement is legally bound to provide products that are suitable, but which may not be the very best for you.” [19]

Right or wrong, technology has brought financial advisors into your home. There are many companies that provide online financial services. One list of online brokers who work with the American Stock Exchange, NASDAQ, is available at: http://www.nasdaq.com/investing/online-brokers/.[20] The list allows you to compare several brokers at a glance.

Once again, we cannot express enough the importance of working with someone on your financial portfolio.

Financial Investments After Retirement: Tread Very Carefully

One of the reasons it is good to have a financial advisor or investor is that many seniors start forgetting things as they age. It’s good to have someone who you have developed a long-term relationship with and whom you trust to help manage your finances. Your financial advisor should know, in advance, what level of risk you are willing to engage. The older we get, the less risk we should take.

Even when you have an advisor, there are some tips that all seniors who are thinking about investing in the stock market or other ventures should know. Kiplinger recommends seniors think strongly about one of two asset-allocation strategies that make safety a premium – either a *bucket plan* or a *cover the basics* approach (Kristof, 2015):

“The bucket formula essentially splits your savings into three pieces, which will be used in the early, middle and late stages of retirement. The cover-the-basics approach aims to match your fixed expenses with fixed sources of income, such as Social Security, pensions and immediate annuities. The rest of your assets are invested to provide income for non-necessities, such as travel and entertainment, which presumably can be postponed during a stock market downturn.”

---

[19] How To Find A Financial Advisor. US. News Money. (n.d.) Retrieved 17 Oct 2016 from http://money.usnews.com/money/personal-finance/financial-advisors/articles/2014/02/26/how-to-find-a-financial-advisor-if-youre-not-rich
[20] Online Broker Partners. NASDAQ. Retrieved 17 Oct 2016 from http://www.nasdaq.com/investing/online-brokers/

US News and World Report recommends seven low-risk, high-reward strategies for seniors (Rose, 2016):

1. Real estate investment trusts
2. Dividend-paying stocks
3. Peer-to-peer lending
4. Municipal bonds
5. Annuities
6. U.S. Treasury notes and bonds
7. Treasury-inflation protected securities.

Everyone should have a plan for the latter part of life. This plan includes sharing your information with a trusted family member or friend on financial details and creating protective, legal documents. We need living wills, long-term care, disability, health proxies and life insurance.

Discuss Your Finances with a Trusted Partner

Money is often one of those issues we do not like to discuss with anyone, especially if we are in debt or have made other bad decisions. Yet, it's particularly important as you age to include at least one other person in your financial affairs. If you don't, your loved ones may suffer unnecessary burdens after you die.

Discussing your finances with a trusted partner also has the added advantage of helping you stay accountable, particularly when you are trying to live the dfree® lifestyle. Sharing your plans, goals and strategies also can add protection against financial scams and con artists – as an additional person will be alert and sensitive to protecting your investments. If you have a financial advisor, introduce your trusted partner – also known as a financial agent – to your advisor and consider legal documents that allow that person to make decisions on your behalf under certain circumstances.

When you discuss your financial situation, make sure you share all relevant information including where you keep important account numbers and access codes. For this reason, take time to decide who you can really trust with such important information and who will act on your behalf if you become incapacitated or die. This is extremely important when it comes to medical matters as well.

Living Wills, Health Proxies and Other Necessary Tools

It is important that you don't leave the challenge of deciding how you want to receive care to your family. Take time to make your desires known, in writing, and leave the necessary resources to carry out your wishes. Make no mistake, there will come a time in life when you will need someone else to conduct your business. Of course, we know that we all will die. Unfortunately, most of us are not used to discussing death with loved ones while we are alive and we have not discovered a way to share our wishes from the morgue or the funeral home table! Remove the stress from your family, friends and community by leaving explicit instruction for your care.

Many people believe if something happens to them their family knows what to do. Unfortunately, many families have experienced additional stress over the decisions concerning their loved one's care.

For example, a man fathered nine children with three different mothers. The man told his eldest daughters to make all the arrangements for his care. He later married a long-time friend and asked that person to assist him with his care and to ensure his wishes were carried out. When the father became incapacitated, the eldest son took over the father's care, which was contrary to the desires he had shared with his daughters and wife. There were several family blow-outs in the hospital room during his illness. In the end the father, who wished not to live in a vegetative state, was placed on life support for 338 days.

Living Wills

Be explicit regarding your care for if you become incapacitated or die. Put your instructions in writing so there is no debate concerning your desires. That is what a living will does. You need a living will or an advance health care directive.

A living will documents your preference for your medical care in circumstances where you are unable to speak or comprehend because of mental incapacity. The will includes which medical procedures and/or life-sustaining techniques you are willing or unwilling to engage in. Your doctors and loved ones would appreciate your consideration in eliminating the doubts and fear they may encounter when there is no directive. Please note, a living will is a necessity for everyone regardless of age. Do not hesitate, thinking you have time to do this later; you may not. The arguments and ill feelings that often arise over the decision to resuscitate someone destroy relationships. A living will is not required in the case of an DNR (Do Not Resuscitate order) but it removes any doubt regarding your wishes. Also, your preferences regarding organ donation should be a part of your living will.

The living will is one element to ensure your wishes are understood when you can no longer manage things for yourself, but also consider assigning someone the role of your health proxy or health care agent. This is someone you trust with your life. Do not get caught up in your emotions to avoid hurting someone's feelings because you select a child over a spouse, or one child over another or a friend over a family member. You know who understands you best. Assign this responsibility to someone who would respond to your care as you would respond.

A living will may not cover every situation you may encounter. Therefore, your health care agent is your voice of reason when it comes to your care. If we browse the web or newspaper articles, we will find instances where there was no living will or health care directive and the family is involved in court battles over the care of their loved one. Show your family you cared, paid attention and took care of the details in order to reduce their stress.

Next, we must discuss insurance. This is a huge discussion that cannot adequately be covered here, but Dr. Soaries' book provides greater detail in this area. We will review the type of insurances you need to reduce stress in your life. We will divide the insurances into categories, as it is in the dfree® lifestyle *12 Steps to Financial Freedom Workbook.* [21]

Disability Insurance: Most employers provide "short-term" disability, better known by many as "sick leave". Individuals have to secure "long-term" disability to supplement income for disability that extends the coverage of short-term. Disability insurance replaces a pre-determined portion of an individual's income if the person is unable to work. It is sad that many employees do not take advantage of long-term disability believing, "it will never happen to me." Remember, it is more likely that a person will become disabled before they turn 65 than they will die before 65!

Homeowners, Renters and Condo Insurance:

The mortgage company requires owners to secure homeowners insurance even though many people are reluctant to insure their homes. That insurance protects them because if something happens to your home, they get paid. Natural disasters are becoming more frequent in America -- such as those caused by Superstorm Sandy, and Hurricanes Katrina, Harvey, Irma and Maria – and should have many homeowners and renters reconsidering the value of an insurance policy for their properties. Landlords have coverage on their property, but they do not cover your personal belongings so you

[21] Soaries Jr., DeForest B. *Say Yes to No Debt: 12 Steps to Financial Freedom Workbook.* Urban Ministries Inc. 2016.

need coverage. Many are shocked at how reasonable renters insurance can be. Condo owners are similar to renters but they own their individual units. The condo association has insurance on the building, but your personal property and personal liability is not covered. If you have a policy, read it and understand what is and is not covered.

Auto Insurance: The law requires automobile insurance however it does not regulate how much coverage is adequate to cover damage to your vehicle. Make sure you have adequate insurance. Too many people purchase low-cost insurance and, when something happens, they are surprised by their low-cost payout. Know the law of your state. Know what minimum coverage is and what it covers. Know what other coverage is available and how much it costs. Finally, identify what you are protecting in your policy. You want enough insurance to cover the cost of a new version of the car that you are currently driving. Should your car be completely destroyed your insurance should give you enough money to but the current year of your car despite the age of your original car.

Professional Liability Insurance: This is coverage for specialist in various professions to protect them from liability. If you are visible to the public in your profession, you need liability insurance. It protects you from liability associated with what you say and do as a professional. Your employer may provide coverage for your work however, if you share your skill or advice outside the workplace as a professional, you could be liable. Cover yourself.

Life Insurance: Life insurance is coverage for you and your loved ones. Many use life insurance as inheritance insurance. This insurance provides a payout to your designee at the time of your death. There are many types of life insurance policies, including term and whole life. Please work with a licensed professional to research the best policy for you.

How much insurance do you need? Some financial experts encourage you to take out a policy that pays ten times your present annual salary. Another formula for calculating how much life insurance you need is called the *DIME* or Debt, Income, Mortgage, Education method. It's simply the sum of your outstanding debt, income replacement for your family and survivors, the balance of your mortgage, and the approximate cost of your children's college education.[22]

[22] Soaries Jr., DeForest B.. Say Yes to No Debt: 12 Steps to Financial Freedom (p. 129). Zondervan. Kindle Edition.

Reverse Mortgage

Another product that is not insurance but is a different kind of mortgage is known as the "reverse" mortgage. The U.S. government through the Department of Housing and Urban Development (HUD) in conjunction with the National Council on Aging explains The Home Equity Conversion Mortgage (HECM), which is FHA's reverse mortgage program. This program enables you to withdraw some of the equity in your home. The HECM is a safe plan that can give older Americans greater financial security.

What is a reverse mortgage? A reverse mortgage is a special type of home loan that lets you convert a portion of the equity in your home into cash. The equity that you built up over years of making mortgage payments can be paid to you. However, unlike a traditional home equity loan or second mortgage, HECM borrowers do not have to repay the HECM loan until the borrowers no longer use the home as their principal residence or fail to meet the obligations of the mortgage. You can also use a HECM to purchase a primary residence, if you are able to use cash on hand to pay the difference between the HECM proceeds and the sales price plus closing costs for the property you are purchasing. However, reverse mortgages can become a pitfall for heirs, who may have to pay off the mortgage to inherit the home.

Once again, please contact a professional to discuss these options. HUD provides detailed information on the reverse mortgage program on their website, http://portal.hud.gov/hudportal/HUD?src=/program_offices/housing/sfh/hecm/rmtopten.

Estate Planning

Finally, estate planning is our last nugget to minimizing stress. You need a will, and estate planning assists you in creating this important document. Estate planning is the process of anticipating and arranging for the disposal of an estate. A will is a legal document that: defines who will receive your assets; details who will become the executor (the person responsible for handling the estate); describes disbursement of assets; and, outlines numerous other issues. The dfree® workbook describes with detail all you will need to map out a process for estate planning. Estate planners report that as many as 70 percent of Americans each year die without having a will in place.[23] Please, don't be one of them.

---

[23] Soaries Jr., DeForest B.. Say Yes to No Debt: 12 Steps to Financial Freedom (p. 131). Zondervan. Kindle Edition.

Don't lose sight of the ultimate goal, which is to live dfree®. We have covered retirement, insurance, wills and health directives, which are all necessary. Even in this careful planning, don't lose sight of your prime focus on eliminating debt, delinquency and deficits. We must balance all of this to free ourselves from the stronghold of financial bondage.

There was a young woman in her thirties. She lived most of her life between low and middle class, by society standards. She had managed, without government support, to maintain her lifestyle and help her child. On the outside she looked like she was making bricks with straws, but on the inside she had subjected herself to a mindset of poverty. She celebrated a layoff from her company because she knew unemployment would last six months. During that time she could pay less in tuition for her child's private school because the school based its rates on an income scale. She had decided that, when her son was ready to go to college, she would get a wage job so he would qualify for scholarships and grants. She had no savings for his college nor anything else. She was living beyond paycheck to paycheck, absorbed in a cycle of borrowing from family and friends and floating checks. (Before banks improved their technology, you could float checks or write a check from one account and use another check to pay it before the original check reached the bank.)

In her forties, she realized how she had limited her potential because of her poverty mindset. She recognized her potential to earn a six-figure income that would not require floating checks, student loans and grants nor borrowing. However, she felt she had learned all of this too late. It wasn't too late. She returned to school. She earned a bachelor's and Masters of Arts, started her own business and started speaking in public forums. This young woman, now reaching middle-age, learned she had a natural gift for presenting. In her late forties, she made her first home purchase.

As she entered her fifties, she was still working to recover from the many pitfalls she endured because of her poverty mindset.

The Poverty Mindset

Too many of us today suffer from the poverty mindset that is pervasive in American culture. Payday lenders, title loan lenders, rent-a-centers, and check cashing businesses thrive on the poverty mindset!

Too many people have bought into a poverty mindset. Then, they rationalize their circumstances and believe it is the only way to survive. The dfree® Financial Freedom Movement helps people adjust their attitudes and focus on better options. We focus on those who have lowered their own expectations and standards for living because of their socioeconomic status because we know they have the potential to do better. Acknowledging our acceptance of living beneath our financial potential is a necessary step in maintaining our focus.

dfree®'s focus is financial freedom. Freedom requires a change in our mindset. We must maintain our momentum on a focused freedom. We must accumulate assets, and we must manage debt, stop delinquency and live within our means to avoid deficit-living. We must maximize our potential to produce. We must strive forward.

Please do not become discouraged. Be encouraged. There are so many tools and resources available to assist you in this journey. Let's get busy making the change. Consider the serenity prayer, "God, grant me the serenity to accept the things I cannot change, Courage to change the things I can, And wisdom to know the difference."

Level 4: Give Back

The final level completes the process of dfree® living and celebrates the joy of financial freedom. Properly investing your resources -- money, time, abilities and possessions -- allows you to experience the true bounty of your riches and to share them with others. Many people at this level mentor others, teach dfree® principles to groups, or ignite the dfree® movement at their churches.

In closing, we'll share a powerful story of a community that is so focused on helping its members, the community has almost eradicated a major health problem.

In Malcolm Gladwell's book, Outliers, he opens with the story of a village in Pennsylvania called Roseto. Roseto is a close-knit community that experienced a low rate of heart disease. It was so small that the medical community and scientists wanted to know why. They decided to study the small community from 1954 to 1961. The community had no heart attacks, even though medical officials considered the group of individuals to be at high-risk for heart disease, and their death rate by heart disease was below 1 percent.

Researchers found that the culture of Roseto was the culture of the Italian village from which many of the residents had migrated. The cohesiveness of the community reduced the stress factors related to heart disease. They ate sugar, fat, pasta, etc. -- the things known to lead to heart disease -- but they did not have the stressors associated with the disease. The citizens of Roseto took care of the citizens of Roseto. If someone lost their job, the community would care for the family until they could care for themselves again. There was no keeping up with the Joneses; everyone was the Joneses. They lived together in the community. The older generation was revered and incorporated into the community. They did not have to worry about their needs, since it was everyone's responsibility. The people in Roseto died of old age.

Just imagine how America would be improved if, community by community, we adopted the Roseto philosophy of caring for one another?

Recently, there was a documentary about the billionaire, Warren Buffett. It told his life story and about his relationship with money and economics. In this documentary, we journey with Mr. Buffett as he continues to gain more and more assets. While Mr. Buffett is securing a solid financial hold, his wife, Susan, is busy with charitable organizations and supporting underserved and marginalized community members. Mr. Buffett jokes, "As soon as I get it, Susie wants to give it away."

Susie later died from cancer. Mr. Buffett then vows to give away most of his fortune to charity. However, he knows it's more than he who has the capacity to make a difference. Warren Buffett enlists other billionaires to join in the commitment to give to those less fortunate.

You don't have Warren Buffett money but you can help someone else. Proverbs 4:7 reminds us, "Wisdom is the principal thing; therefore, get wisdom: and with all thy getting get understanding." Hopefully, you have learned some techniques, some skills or secured some information that will aide you in supporting this dfree® movement. Now it is time for you to share your knowledge with someone else.

Money is mentioned 130 times in the Bible. It is an essential element to life's journey in whatever form it is secured. Some people think, "money is the root of all evil," but it is the "love of money" that is the root. We must remember that God is the provider of all things, including money, Deuteronomy 8:18.

Our challenge:

1. Apply the principals of dfree® living to your life;
2. Share the story of dfree® with family and friends;
3. Start a group to discuss the elements and power of living dfree®;
4. Make your church or organization a beneficiary in one of your life insurance policies; and,
5. Leave an asset to your church or charity of your choice in your will or trust.

We believe this dfree® movement can be a community movement, a city movement, a state movement which would lead to a country movement and eventually a worldwide movement. Imagine if your community was a dfree® living community. It is possible.

Will you join us in this endeavor to change the world? Who else do you feel will embrace the concepts of dfree® and become good partners with us? Let us know!

Help us share what you have learned with others. Join us in this endeavor to be DFREE®!

Appendix

SOME FACTS ABOUT SENIORS – YOU ARE NOT ALONE!

Did you know?

Times are changing! We are living longer and are healthier than ever before in history. The world is experiencing a profound and irreversible demographic shift in the developed and developing worlds that is unprecedented in human history. Thanks to lower fertility rates and increases in longevity, the number of people age 60 years and over is expected to triple worldwide, from 737 million people in 2009 to 2 billion by 2050.[24]

Did you know?

There was a time in history when one out of ten individuals would live to the age of 65. Today, eight of ten will zoom past the age of 65 and live longer than earlier generations. Technology and medical advances have moved "old" age; 65 is the new 40. (Amen!) The latest U.S. Census Bureau report estimates that, between now and 2050, the population that is 65 and older will more than double while the population under 20 years of age will see almost no growth.[25]

---

[24] Aging, with grace. The American Psychology Association. 11 Nov. 2011. Retrieved 7 Oct 2016. from **http://www.apa.org/monitor/2011/11/ce-corner.aspx**

[25] 'First Time in Human History': People 65 and Older Will Outnumber Children Under 5. CNS News. 31 Mar. 2016. Retrieved 7 Oct 2016 from http://cnsnews.com/news/article/terence-p-jeffrey/first-time-human-history-global-population-over-65-poised-pass

Did you know?

Many individuals over 65 find themselves returning to the workforce after retirement. Many individuals who have retired from companies to which they gave over 20 years of service find themselves starting new careers.

Did you know?

As the workforce has changed, the number of senior adults impacted by consumer debt has increased. National Council on Aging statistics' show the following for senior adults living on a fixed income:

- Over 25 million Americans age 60+—or roughly 1 in 3 older adults—are economically insecure, living on incomes at or below 250 percent of the federal poverty level.
- 22 percent of married, Social Security recipients and 47% of single recipients aged 65+ depend on Social Security for 90 percent or more of their income.
- Older women typically receive about $4,000 less annually in Social Security than older men due to: lower lifetime earnings; time taken off for caregiving; occupational segregation into lower wage work; and, other issues. Older women of color are even worse off.
- In 2015, the average older adult receiving Supplemental Security Income received just $433 each month.[26]

Did you know?

- In 2013, 61.3 percent of households headed by an adult aged 60+ had some form of debt. Among senior households with debt, the median total debt was $40,900 (Federal Reserve Board).
- One-third of senior households have no money left over each month or are in debt after meeting essential expenses (Institute on Assets and Social Policy).
- One in four senior households with any credit card debt had a balance of at least $7,200 in 2013.

[26] Economic Security Poverty Facts About Aging. National Council on Aging. (n.d.) Retrieved 7 Oct 2016. from https://www.ncoa.org/news/resources-for-reporters/get-the-facts/economic-security-facts/

To Learn More about the
dfree® Financial Freedom Movement, visit
www.mydfree.org and **www.billiondollarpaydown.com**.

Stay Connected!!!
@mydfree

Made in the USA
Monee, IL
05 November 2026

67383933R00033